HOW TO HOLD UP THE MAIL

HOW TO HOLD UP THE MAIL

BY J. U. **GORHAM.** *Being a helpful GUIDE for*
SUBURBANITE *and* COUNTRYMAN
and by which the CITY "SLICKER" *may know the*
Ingenious Art of BOXING *the* POSTAL SERVICE

THE STEPHEN GREENE PRESS

BRATTLEBORO, VT
1973
05301

5-28-74

This book has been produced in the United States of America: composed by The Stephen Greene Press and printed and bound by the Springfield Printing Corpora-tion. It is published by The Stephen Greene Press, Brattleboro, Vermont 05301.

Library of Congress Catalog Card Number: 73-82744
International Standard Book Number: 0-8289-0191-0
73 74 75 76 77 78 79 9 8 7 6 5 4 3 2 1

✳ PREFACE ✳

1814151

There are some of us who, if we *don't* hold up the mail . . . . .

. . . . . don't get any!

❄ HOW TO HOLD UP THE MAIL ❄

From U. S. Postal Regulations, Rural Service:

The Postal Regulations require that patrons must provide and erect at their own expense rural mail boxes which meet official specifications.

.53 Posts and supports

    .531 Construction

        Posts or other supports must be neat and of adequate strength and size. They may not be designed to represent effigies or caricatures that would tend to disparage or ridicule any person. The box may be attached to a fixed or a movable arm.

.54 Location

        Rural boxes must be placed so that they may be safely and conveniently served by carriers without leaving their conveyances . . . .

You can see what the problem is.

Look.

Here's one way to do it.

Sturdy and neat, on a post.

Or that old log that's been hanging around.

Or something left behind.

Why not add a modest decoration here and there?

But the postman would say:

Forget the decor.

Just make it high enough for me to reach.

O. K.

go.

we

Up

High enough now?

But look.
Just when you set it up it starts to lean.

Damn!

It's that old devil ditch that does it.

What is this strange attraction that
mail boxes have for a ditch?

Don't let them fall for it—

Fight Back
with firm
and
bracing
attitudes!

Or pretend to give in.

Over and Out without seeming to.

And the ditch gurgles merrily on.

Or be Constructive.

Everyone likes a real Straight Shooter

or an A-Frame Straddler.

How about these Carpenter's Delight models?

But even so, that ditch is always there, weakening
the best of intentions.

It can keep you awake at night.

And as long as you're awake, you might as well
sneak out—

and add a little
wire here and there.

No one really notices it.

Good old wire.

Here's a front view of the same, so you can
appreciate all the thought and effort
hanging by a thread, so to speak.

Improvisation is another great method.

It's easy to see what came first here,
but then what?

You can always say —

But I haven't finished yet!

As in this Ditch Wader, on its way.

NEVER cross a ditch this way.

It's too upsetting.

And unnerving.

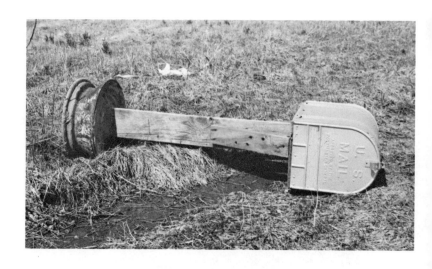

When it happens, you lose your head.

You grab anything, stick or stone,

wire or bone! Hammer! Nails! Run!

To the rescue!

SAVED!

SAVED AGAIN!

Of course, you can just set it up for good and all, and forget it.

But this suggests Another Way . . . .

The Weighty Approach, or . . . .

(Here's a stubborn one. Just try to move THAT.)

26

. . . . the Milky Way.

But notez bien,
as the poet said—

We're on the verge
of a whole new
Art Form—

PLUMBING!

Wow!

More!!

O reserved and stately pipes!

Still more!
Two superb examples of the
Change of Mind School.

These deserve real study.

Don't turn the page too quickly.

Curves, too!

Aahh . . . .

Softly flowing,

Gently reaching,
Graceful curves.

1814151

Whee!

And good old Z!

Now, here's Plumbing Plus.

Hello, Wheels.

Old wheels, new wheels, we love you all!

Wooden wheels, metal wheels,

You're what we've been looking for!

And here we have wheels and what goes with them:

Wheels Masterpiece A.

Wheels Masterpiece B.

(Note the devices used to restrain wheelish activity.)

NOW: The Wheel with Work Implement.

We cultivate—

The plow.

And how!

And PUMPS.

shortish   tallish

mannish   boyish

PUMPS!

Here's to pumps!

More Found Objects:

An overturned
something.

Perhaps you recognize it.

An overturned branch.

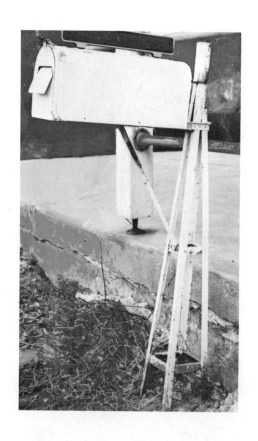

What appears to be a tripod
is actually a—

        quadpod?

A fine old post,
sawed off.

More Founds:

This one is a real gasser,
if I do say so.

Whatever this is,
it is a splendid example of it!

And lastly—two triumphs in the
Found Objects class:

The delicious Aeolian Harp model,

and this.

Let's face it though,
Finding Objects can be a big cover up

for doing nothing and calling it something.

Like this.

Or this.

Though that old oaken barrel gets to you.

When you think of the work
that some people go to,
digging,
hammering,
and what not—

and then see how others

just PLANT
their mailboxes
on ANYTHING
and get away with it—

It makes you want to yell,

"NO FAIR!"

Where would these be

without a house   or a tree

or the electric company?

Here's a little Extra, just to change the pace —
a sort of Urban Growth.

Single creations aren't the only way it's done.

Here we have a group project,

Solid Citizens at a Community Weigh-In.

And here is one of your typical
Lower Middle Income Groups.

Sometimes you'll see a couple of Old Pals—

or New Pals.

Or an attempt to reconcile Outright Individualists.

Or those under Group Therapy

or Leftward Leaners.

Or a Bunch of Drunks.

We pause now for a little sadness,
or nostalgia, or what have you—

as we see what happens when someone moves away . . . .

. . . . and someone else moves in.

But don't be downhearted.

Before I close
let me leave you with this little message
to help you through your day:

HI!

An ancient philosopher once said that—

Life is full of twists and turns

in which lurks great irony.

So it's best we stay close to nature,

linked by all those things we like:

Finding each other,

building homes,

raising families,

watering flowers

and lighting the way

for all the birds

and the little animals.

So long.

❄ APPENDIX ❄

FOR THOSE WHO WANT MORE

Here are some more, all different, that I couldn't quite fit into the story but hadn't the heart to abandon.

All of the mail box holders in this book were found in one area, about 75 miles from New York City. No attempt was made to search out unusual or strange ones—they were just there. Travel a short distance away from the population crush and you'll see them too.

THE WOODLAND LURCHER

THE WOODLAND GRAPPLER

THE WING DING

THE BASHFUL BRIDE

THE BRICKIUP

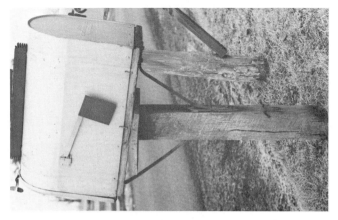

THE DOUBTING THOMAS

THE STURDIO

THE WHEELY DEALER

93

THE ANGLE   THE ROADSIDE FANCY   THE FENCY FANCY

THE CRISS CROSS

THE SQUARE P. IN A ROUND H.

THE SPIRIT OF '76

THE PERFECT

THE SAUCY HOLD-OUT

THE MIXED MARRIAGE

THE POTTED PLANT

THE FLIRTY SKIRTY

THE JOLLY POT

THE MARTIAN
ROVERS

THE BOLTS
AND ALL

THE FURTHER
REACHES

N IS FOR REDUNDANCE

THE DACHSY

THE BOXY

THE ROCKSY

THE SPY

THE TEA FOR TWO

THE TWO FOR TEA

THE FLAT OUT WITH HOLES

THE WELL-DRESSED RELATION

THE SCREWTINIZER

THE F. THAT BLOOM
IN THE S.,
TRA-LA

THE ARTIST

THE HOOP IN THE HOLLOW

THE BOARDING HOUSE REACH

THE PIGGY PEN

THE OUTCASTS OF SNOWY FLAT

104

THE OVERACHIEVER

THE SLAP AND DASH

THE "SAY AAHH"

THE GRIP OF IRON

THE VENUSIAN GRASSHOPPER

THE WEE BARN

THE HARD WAY

THE MAIL BIRD

THE EAGER ENTRIES

THE STRANGE ATTACHMENTS   THE WEE FOR WICTORY

THE BROKEN ANKLE

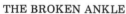

THE STARS AND STRIPES
FOREVER

THE PURLOINED PILINGS

THE TREEHOUSE

THE WAYWARD BEDPOST

THE CHIP

AND THE OLD
BLOCK

110

THE HAYWIRE

THE MUSHROOMS

THE HEFTY S.

THE TOURNIQUET

THE SAVING BRACE

THE HEAVYWEIGHT PRETENDER

THE THREE LEGGED
RACE

THE BRAIN

THE BITS AND PIECES

THE SNAKEY UPRISING

THE GENERATION GAP

THE SHAKY SCROLL

114

THE TUBBY

THE ROMANTIC

THE AUSTRALIAN CRAWL

THE COLONIAL MEMORY

THE WHATNOT

THE NOSEY CYCLOPS

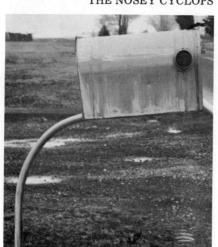

THE CURLY

THE SCOTCH WATCH

THE TEN SECONDS
FROM LIFTOFF
AND COUNTING

17

THE STRANGE CONNECTION

THE LITTLE FOL DE ROL

THE WILDWOOD
HUSKY

11

THE STRANGE FRUIT

THE HANDSOME
OUTRIDER

THE STUMPED

19

THE KEG O' MY HEART

THE YODELER AND THE CLAM

THE MOTHER HENS

THE DRUM MAJOR

THUS, ON AND ON—
   through snow, through rain, through
      heat, through gloom of night
         —DOWN THE LONG,
            LONG ROAD TO THE
                     POST OFFICE.